MW01533253

INTRODUCTION

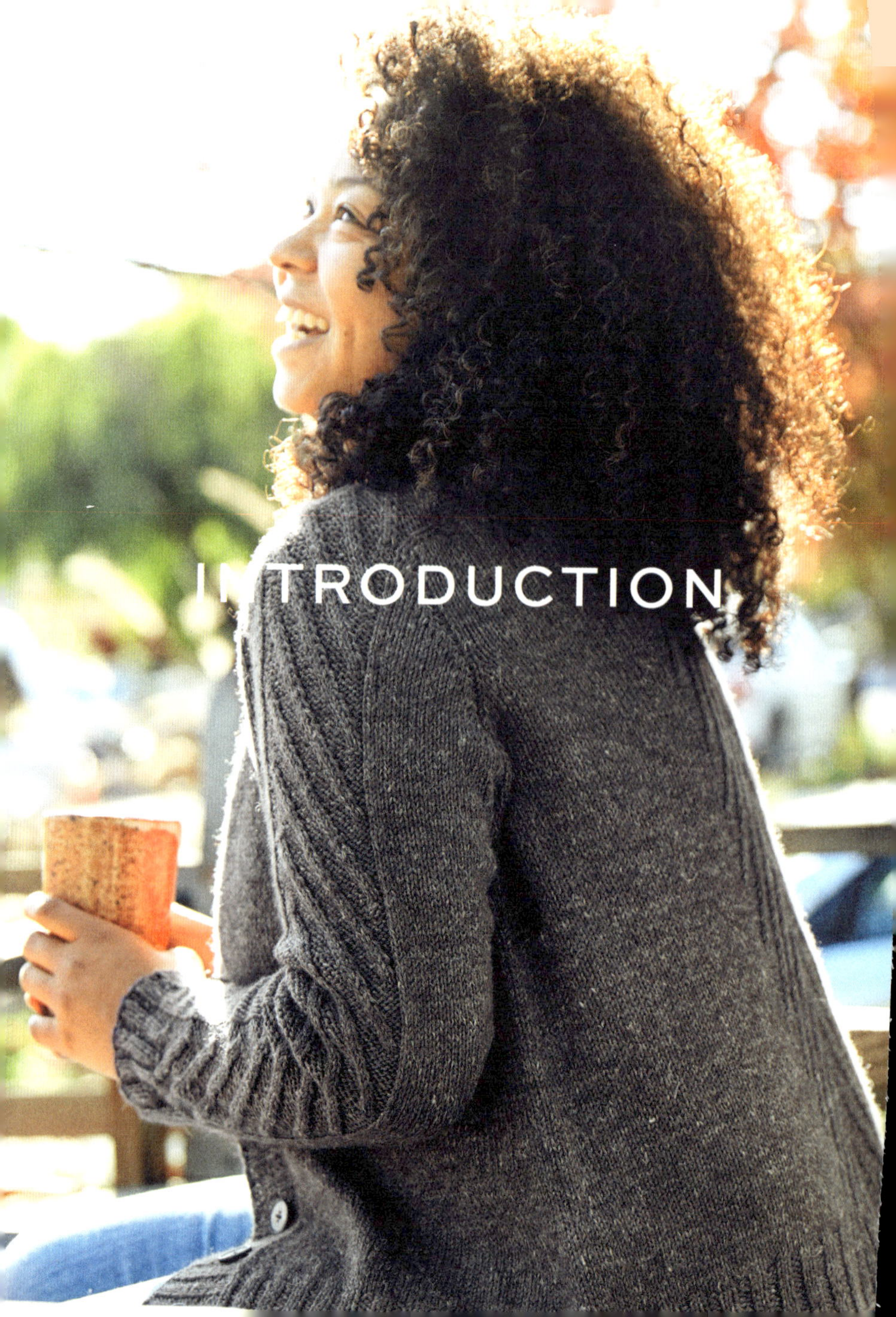

I T'S AS SIMPLE AS THE COOL SIDE OF A PILLOW, a window opened, those favorite sandals fished out of the closet. As the days grow longer, we crave the new. We're wiggling our toes and marveling that we get to be warm again. As nature releases its spectacular color, we want to create something brand new, too.

This Field Guide celebrates the transition, the welcome moment when we see where we've been and look forward to what lies ahead. We are lucky to have a designer for this Field Guide who sets us up with extraordinary projects that suit this season of renewal.

We have been admiring Carol Feller's work for over a decade. During that time she has created more than 300 designs. True expertise comes from such experience—developing ideas, resolving their challenges, and mining their potential.

Carol grew up in Ireland in a family with a long history of crafting. Her mother sewed many of her clothes. Her grandmother was an expert knitter, and her aunt ran a yarn shop in Dublin. Carol learned to knit in primary school, and fondly recalls making cardigans for her dolls and occasionally for herself during her growing-up years.

Today Carol revels in the engineering of a handknit design. She trained first as a textile artist, then as a structural engineer, so she is uniquely attuned to the beauty of a fabric and also to structure, that crucial component of design. What holds up? What works?

Again and again, hers are the designs that we stop to study—they are eternally interesting, subtle, and clever. The art is in the details, and as knitters, we delight in discovering them.

In this Field Guide, Carol offers us four fresh and artful designs full of clever bits and worked in a blend of merino, yak, and linen called Nua Sport—a yarn that elegantly balances warmth, lightness, strength, and drape.

We have a hat with ribbing that curves and arches; a wrap with cables that zig and zag and swirl like rivulets emerging in spring rains, a top with a unique button closure, and a superbly constructed cardigan with cables that intersect at dramatic angles. The question is where to begin?

Love,

Kay   Ann

Although Carol is inspired by Ireland's rich traditions and landscape, she strives to interpret them through a modern lens.

TRANSOM CARDIGAN

Design by

Carol Feller

FESTOONED WITH GRAPHIC DIAGONAL CABLES, this is a cardigan that works as well for an evening out on the town as it does over plaid PJ bottoms for a cozy night in. It is an elegant, architectural design, a show-stopper, but one in which nothing is done just for show.

The knitting begins with the central back panel that spans the width of the saddle shoulders. From there, you pick up stitches from each side and work the saddle. When both saddles are complete, you pick up stitches along the side edges and work the yoke and sleeve with a short-row set-in sleeve method. Then you finish the body and sleeves separately from the top down. The final touch: a shaped collar.

KNITTED MEASUREMENTS

Bust: 35½ (38½, 42½, 45) (48, 51¾, 55¼) (57½, 60½, 64¼)" [90 (98, 108, 114.5) (122, 131.5, 140.5) (146, 153.5, 163) cm], buttoned

Length: 21¾ (22¼, 23, 23½) (24, 24¾, 25¼) (25¾, 26¼, 26½)" [55 (56.5, 58.5, 59.5) (61, 63, 64) (65.5, 66.5, 67.5) cm]

SIZES

To fit bust sizes 30-33 (33-36, 37-40, 40-43, 43-46, 46-49, 50-53, 52-55, 55-58, 59-62)" [76-84 (84-91.5, 94-101.5, 101.5-109, 109-117, 117-124.5, 127-134.5, 132-139.5, 139.5-147.5, 150-157.5) cm]

MATERIALS

— Nua by Stolen Stitches [50 g skeins, each approx 153 yds (140 m), 60% merino wool, 20% yak, 20% linen]: 8 (9, 9, 10, 11, 11, 12, 12, 13, 14) skeins August Storms
— Size US 6 (4 mm) circular needle, 32" (80 cm) long or longer, and double-pointed needles (set of 4 or 5), or size needed to achieve gauge
— Stitch markers
— Cable needle
— Stitch holders or waste yarn
— 6 buttons, ¾" (19 mm) diameter

GAUGE

21 sts and 30 rows = 4" (10 cm) over stockinette stitch

27 sts and 30 rows = 4" (10 cm) over Right or Left Diagonal Cable

NOTES

This cardigan is worked in one piece from the top down. The back panel is worked first from the center out for each side and the saddles are placed on holders. Next, stitches are picked up for the back and worked to the underarms, with wrap-and-turn short-row shaping for the shoulders. The fronts are worked in a similar manner. The back and fronts are then joined and the body is worked to the bottom. Sleeve stitches are picked up from the armholes at each side of the held saddle stitches and the cap is shaped using wrap-and-turn short rows; the sleeve is then worked in the round to the cuff. Stitches are picked up for the front bands/collar and the collar is shaped using German short rows.

You may work the Right and Left Diagonal Cables from either the text or the charts. The flat versions are worked for the body and sleeve caps; the circular versions are worked for the sleeves.

SPECIAL TECHNIQUES

Wrap-and-Turn Short Rows: Short-row shaping allows you to work extra rows on a particular section of your knitting, such as the back neck, without adding rows to the entire piece. Work short rows using w&t as instructed, then when indicated, work wraps together with wrapped sts as follows: If working on a knit st, insert right needle into the wrap from below, then into wrapped st and knit them together. If working on a purl st, lift wrap onto left needle, then work it together with wrapped st. When working sleeve cap shaping, do not work wraps together with wrapped stitches; they form a faux seamline between the sleeves and the front and back.

German Short Rows: Work the number of stitches indicated in the pattern, turn work. With the yarn in front, slip the first stitch purlwise, then pull the yarn tightly up and over the needle so that the two legs of the stitch below the slipped stitch are showing; this creates a Double Stitch (DS) on the right needle. If the next stitch to be worked is a purl stitch, bring the yarn back around to the front, ready to purl; if the next stitch is a knit stitch, keep the yarn to the back, ready to knit. When you come to the gap created by the DS on the next row, knit or purl the two legs of the DS together to close the DS, depending on whether the stitch is to be a knit stitch or a purl stitch. The two legs of the DS will always be counted as a single stitch.

Single Row Buttonhole: Slip 1 stitch with yarn in front, [slip 1 stitch with yarn in back, pass first slipped stitch over second slipped stitch to bind off 1 stitch] 3 times; slip resulting stitch back to left-hand needle, turn; cast on 4 stitches using cable cast-on, turn; slip 1 stitch from left-hand needle to right-hand needle and pass last cast-on stitch over it.

SPECIAL ABBREVIATIONS

DS (Double Stitch): See Special Techniques, German Short Rows.

M1L: (make 1 left) Insert left needle from front to back under horizontal strand between stitch just worked and the next stitch on the left needle. Knit this strand through the back loop. One stitch has been increased.

M1PL: (make 1 purlwise, left) Insert left needle from front to back under horizontal strand between stitch just worked and the next stitch on the left needle. Purl this strand through the back loop. One stitch has been increased.

M1PR: (make 1 purlwise, right) Insert left needle from back to front under horizontal strand between stitch just worked and the next stitch on the left needle. Purl this strand through the front loop. One stitch has been increased.

M1R: (make 1 right) Insert left needle from back to front under horizontal strand between stitch just worked and the next stitch on the left needle. Knit this strand through the front loop. One stitch has been increased.

w&t: Wrap and turn. On a knit row, move yarn to the front of work, slip next stitch, take yarn to the back of work, slip wrapped stitch to left needle. Turn work. On a purl row, move yarn to the back of work, slip next stitch, bring yarn to the front of work, slip wrapped stitch back to left needle, turn work.

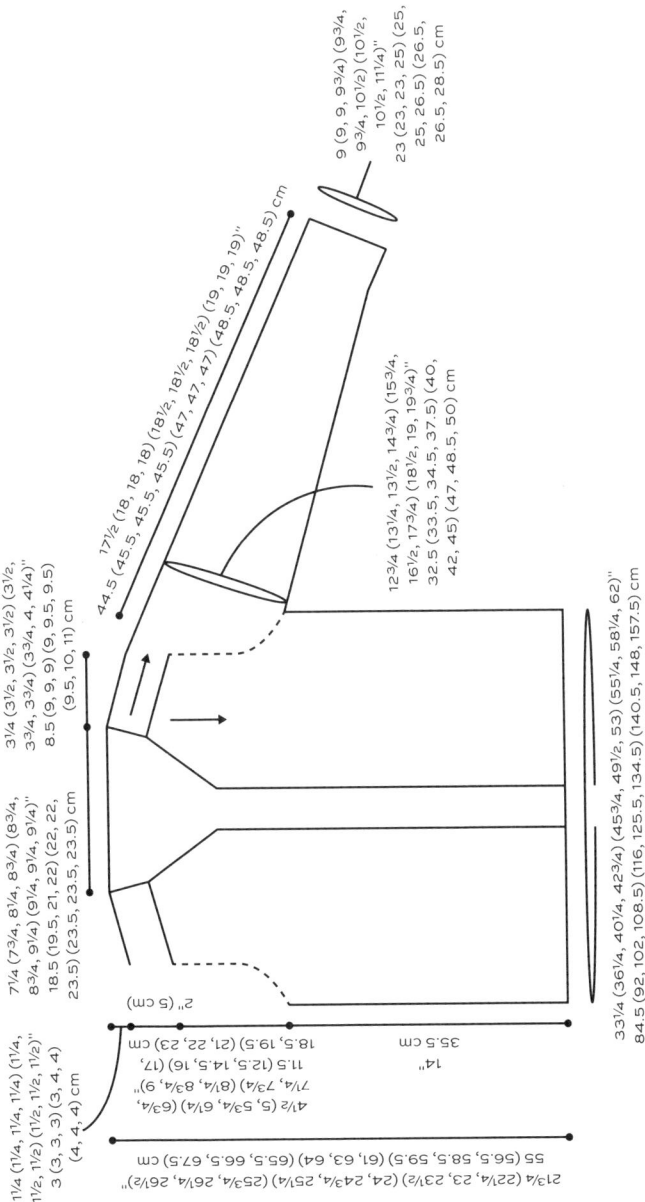

9 (9, 9, 9¾) (9¾, 9¾, 10½) (10½, 11¼)"
23 (23, 23, 25) (25, 25, 26.5) (26.5, 28.5) cm

12¾ (13¼, 13½, 14¾) (15¾, 16½, 17¾) (18½, 19, 19¾)"
32.5 (33.5, 34.5, 37.5) (40, 42, 45) (47, 48.5, 50) cm

17½ (18, 18, 18) (18½, 18½, 18½) (19, 19, 19)"
44.5 (45.5, 45.5, 45.5) (47, 47, 47) (48.5, 48.5, 48.5) cm

3¼ (3½, 3½, 3½) (3½, 3¾, 3¾) (3¾, 4, 4¼)"
8.5 (9, 9, 9) (9, 9.5, 9.5) (9.5, 10, 11) cm

7¼ (7¾, 8¼, 8¾) (8¾, 8¾, 9¼) (9¼, 9¼, 9¼)"
18.5 (19.5, 21, 22) (22, 22, 23.5) (23.5, 23.5, 23.5) cm

33¼ (36¼, 40¼, 42¾) (45¾, 49½, 53) (55¼, 58¼, 62)"
84.5 (92, 102, 108.5) (116, 125.5, 134.5) (140.5, 148, 157.5) cm

2" (5 cm)

1¼ (1¼, 1¼, 1¼) (1¼, 1½, 1½, 1½) (1½, 1½)"
3 (3, 3, 3) (3, 4, 4) (4, 4, 4) cm

18.5, 19.5) (21, 22, 23) cm
11.5 (12.5, 14.5, 16) (17, 7¼, 7¾) (8¼, 8¾, 9)"
4½ (5, 5¾, 6¼) (6¾, 14"
35.5 cm

21¾ (22¾, 23, 23½) (24, 24½, 25¼) (25¾, 26¼, 26½)"
55 (56.5, 58.5, 59.5) (61, 63, 64) (65.5, 66.5, 67.5) cm

STITCH PATTERNS

Flat 2×2 Rib (multiple of 4 sts + 2)

— *Row 1 (RS):* *K2, p2; rep from * to last 2 sts, k2.

— *Row 2:* *P2, k2; rep from * to last 2 sts, p2.

— Rep Rows 1 and 2 for Flat 2×2 Rib.

Circular 2×2 Rib (multiple of 4 sts)

— *All Rnds:* *K2, p2; rep from * to end.

Flat Right Diagonal Cable

(multiple of 6 sts + 3)

— *Row 1 (RS):* P6, *2/1 RPC, p3; rep from * to last 3 sts, 2/1 RPC.

— *Rows 2, 4, 6, 8, and 10:* Knit the k sts and purl the p sts as they face you.

— *Row 3:* P5, *2/1 RPC, p3; rep from * to last 4 sts, 2/1 RPC, p1.

— *Row 5:* P4, *2/1 RPC, p3; rep from * to last 5 sts, 2/1 RPC, p2.

— *Row 7:* P3, *2/1 RPC, p3; rep from * to end.

— *Row 9:* P2, *2/1 RPC, p3; rep from * to last st, p1.

— *Row 11:* P1, *2/1 RPC, p3; rep from * to last 2 sts, p2.

— *Row 12:* P2, *k4, p2; rep from * to last st, k1.

— Rep Rows 1–12 for Flat Right Diagonal Cable.

Circular Right Diagonal Cable

(multiple of 6 sts + 3)

— *Rnd 1:* P6, *2/1 RPC, p3; rep from * to last 3 sts, 2/1 RPC .

— *Rnds 2, 4, 6, 8, and 10:* Knit the knit sts and purl the purl sts as they face you.

— *Rnd 3:* P5, *2/1 RPC, p3; rep from * to last 4 sts, 2/1 RPC, p1.

— *Rnd 5:* P4, *2/1 RPC, p3; rep from * to last 5 sts, 2/1 RPC, p2.

— *Rnd 7:* P3, *2/1 RPC, p3; rep from * to end.

— *Rnd 9:* P2, *2/1 RPC, p3; rep from * to last st, p1.

— *Rnd 11:* P1, *2/1 RPC, p3; rep from * to last 2 sts, p2.

— *Rnd 12:* P1, *k2, p4; rep from * to last 2 sts, k2.

— Rep Rnds 1–12 for Circular Right Diagonal Cable.

Flat Left Diagonal Cable

(multiple of 6 sts + 3)

— *Row 1 (RS):* *2/1 LPC, p3; rep from * to last 3 sts, p3.

— *Rows 2, 4, 6, 8, and 10:* Knit the knit sts and purl the purl sts as they face you.

— *Row 3:* P1, *2/1 LPC, p3; rep from * to last 2 sts, p2.

— *Row 5:* P2, *2/1 LPC, p3; rep from * to last st, p1.
— *Row 7:* P3, *2/1 LPC, p3; rep from * to end.
— *Row 9:* P4, *2/1 LPC, p3; rep from * to last 5 sts, 2/1 LPC p2.
— *Row 11:* P5, *2/1 LPC, p3; rep from * to last 4 sts, 2/1 LPC, p1.
— *Row 12:* K1, *p2, k4; rep from * to last 2 sts, p2.
— Rep Rows 1–12 for Flat Left Diagonal Cable.

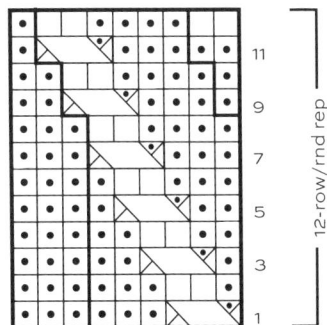

Circular Left Diagonal Cable

(multiple of 6 sts + 3)

— *Rnd 1:* 2/1 LPC, p3; rep from * to last 3 sts, p3.
— *Rnds 2, 4, 6, 8, and 10:* Knit the knit sts and purl the purl sts as they face you.
— *Rnd 3:* P1, *2/1 LPC, p3; rep from * to last 2 sts, p2.
— *Rnd 5:* P2, *2/1 LPC, p3; rep from * to last st, p1.
— *Rnd 7:* P3, *2/1 LPC, p3; rep from * to end.
— *Rnd 9:* P4, *2/1 LPC, p3; rep from * to last 5 sts, 2/1 LPC p2.
— *Rnd 11:* P5, *2/1 LPC, p3; rep from * to last 4 sts, 2/1 LPC, p1.
— *Rnd 12:* K2, *p4, k2; rep from * to last st, p1.
— Rep Rnds 1–12 for Circular Left Diagonal Cable.

Right Diagonal Cable

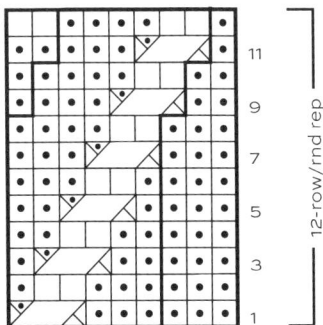

6-st rep

12-row/rnd rep

Left Diagonal Cable

6-st rep

12-row/rnd rep

Knit on RS, purl on WS.

Purl on RS, knit on WS.

2/1 RPC

2/1 LPC

BACK PANEL

— CO 48 (50, 52, 58) (58, 58, 60) (60, 60, 60) sts.
— *Set-Up Row (WS):* P3 (4, 5, 2) (2, 2, 3) (3, 3, 3), pm, k3, [k4, p2] 3 (3, 3, 4) (4, 4, 4) (4, 4, 4) times, [p2, k4] 3 (3, 3, 4) (4, 4, 4) (4, 4, 4) times, k3, pm, p3 (4, 5, 2) (2, 2, 3) (3, 3, 3).
— *Next Row:* Knit to marker, sm, work Flat Right Diagonal Cable over 21 (21, 21, 27) (27, 27, 27) (27, 27, 27) sts, work Left Diagonal Cable over 21 (21, 21, 27) (27, 27, 27) (27, 27, 27) sts, sm, knit to end.
— Work even until piece measures 2" (5 cm), ending with a WS row, making note of last row of pattern worked. Cut yarn and place sts on st holder or waste yarn.

RIGHT SADDLE

— With RS of back panel facing and beg just above sts on hold, pick up and knit 13 sts along short side edge of panel; turn to WS and CO 13 sts using cable CO—26 sts.
— *Set-Up Row (WS):* P2, k1, [p2, k4] 3 times, k3, p2.
— *Next Row:* K2, work Flat Right Diagonal Cable over 21 sts, p1, k2.
— Work even until piece measures 3 (3¼, 3¼, 3¼) (3¼, 3½, 3½) (3½, 3¾, 4)" [7.5 (8.5, 8.5, 8.5) (8.5, 9, 9) (9, 9.5, 10) cm] from picked-up sts, ending with a WS row; note last row of pattern worked. Cut yarn and place sts on st holder or waste yarn.

LEFT SADDLE

— Using cable CO, CO 13 sts, do not turn; with RS of back panel facing and beg at CO edge, pick up and knit 13 sts along remaining short side edge of panel—26 sts.
— *Set-Up Row (WS):* P2, k3, [k4, p2] 3 times, k1, p2.
— *Next Row:* K2, p1, work Flat Left Diagonal Cable over 21 sts, k2.
— Work even until piece measures 3 (3¼, 3¼, 3¼) (3¼, 3½, 3½) (3½, 3¾, 4)" [7.5 (8.5, 8.5) (8.5, 8.5, 9) (9, 9, 9.5, 10) cm] from picked-up sts, ending with a WS row; note last row of pattern worked. Cut yarn and place sts on st holder or waste yarn.

BACK

— With RS of back panel and saddles facing and beg just above sts on hold for left saddle, pick up and knit 17 (18, 18, 18) (18, 20, 20) (20, 21, 22) sts across long back edge of left saddle, pm, work in pattern across back panel sts (beg with next row after last row worked on back panel), pm, pick up and knit 17 (18, 18, 18) (18, 20, 20) (20, 21, 22) sts across long back edge of right saddle—82 (86, 88, 94) (94, 98, 100) (100, 102, 104) sts.

SHAPE SHOULDERS

— *Short Row 1 (WS):* Purl to marker, sm, work to marker, sm, p2, w&t.
— *Short Row 2 (RS)*: Knit to marker, sm, work to marker, sm, k2, w&t.
— *Short Row 3:* Work to wrapped st, work wrap tog with wrapped st, p3, w&t.
— *Short Row 4:* Work to wrapped st, work wrap tog with wrapped st, k3, w&t.
— Rep Short Rows 3 and 4 two (2, 2, 2) (2, 3, 3) (3, 3, 3) more times.
— *Short Row 5:* Work to end, working wrap tog with wrapped st as you come to it.
— *Next Row:* Work to end, working wrap tog with wrapped st as you come to it.
— Work even until piece measures 2¾ (3¼, 3, 3½) (3¼, 3½, 4) (4¼, 4½, 4½)" [7 (8.5, 7.5, 9) (8.5, 9, 10) (11, 11.5, 11.5) cm] from picked-up sts, ending with a WS row.

SHAPE ARMHOLES

— *Inc Row 1 (RS):* K2, M1L, work to last 2 sts, M1R, k2—2 sts inc.
— Work 1 row even.
— Rep last 2 rows 5 (5, 8, 7, 10, 11, 10, 11, 12, 12) more times—94 (98, 106, 110) (116, 122, 122) (124, 128, 130) sts.
— Rep Inc Row 1 once.
— *Inc Row 2 (WS):* P2, M1PL, work to last 2 sts, M1PR, p2—2 sts inc.
— Rep last 2 rows 0 (0, 0, 1) (1, 1, 2) (2, 2, 3) more time(s), making note of last row of pattern worked—98 (102, 110, 118) (124, 130, 134) (136, 140, 146) sts.
— Cut yarn and place sts on st holder or waste yarn.

RIGHT FRONT

— With RS facing, pick up and knit 17 (18, 18, 18) (18, 20, 20) (20, 21, 22) sts along front edge of right saddle.
— *Short Row 1 (WS):* P2, w&t.
— *Short Row 2 (RS)*: Knit to end.
— *Short Row 3:* Purl to wrapped st, work wrap tog with wrapped st, p3, w&t.
— *Short Row 4:* Knit to end.
— Rep Short Rows 3 and 4 two (2, 2, 2) (2, 3, 3) (3, 3, 3) more times.
— *Next Row (WS):* Work to end, working remaining wrap tog with wrapped st as you come to it.

SHAPE NECK AND ARMHOLE

Note: Neck and armhole are shaped at the same time; please read through entire section before beg.

— *Neck Inc Row (RS):* Work to last 2 sts, M1R, k2—1 st inc.
— Purl 1 row.
— Rep last 2 rows 13 (14, 15, 16) (16, 16, 18) (18, 18, 18) more times. AT THE SAME TIME, when piece measures 2¾ (3¼, 3, 3½) (3¼, 3½, 4) (4¼, 4½, 4½)" [7 (8.5, 7.5, 9) (8.5, 9, 10) (11, 11.5, 11.5) cm] from picked-up sts, ending with a WS row, beg armhole shaping as follows:
— *Armhole Inc Row 1 (RS):* K2, M1L, work to end—1 st inc.
— Purl 1 row.
— Rep last 2 rows 5 (5, 8, 7) (10, 11, 10) (11, 12, 12) more times.
— Rep Armhole Inc Row 1 once.
— *Armhole Inc Row 2 (WS):* Work to last 2 sts, M1PL, p2—1 st inc.
— Rep last 2 rows 0 (0, 0, 1) (1, 1, 2) (2, 2, 3) more time(s)—39 (41, 45, 47) (50, 53, 56) (57, 59, 62) sts when all shaping is complete.
— Cut yarn and place sts on st holder or waste yarn.

LEFT FRONT

— With RS facing, pick up and knit 17 (18, 18, 18) (18, 20, 20) (20, 21, 22) sts along front edge of left saddle.
— Purl 1 row.
— *Short Row 1 (RS):* K2, w&t.
— *Short Row 2 (WS):* Purl to end.
— *Short Row 3 (RS):* Knit to wrapped st, work wrap tog with wrapped st, k3, w&t.
— *Short Row 4 (WS):* Purl to end.
— Rep Short Rows 3 and 4 two (2, 2, 2) (2, 3, 3) (3, 3, 3) more times.
— *Next Row (RS):* Work to end, working remaining wrap tog with wrapped st as you come to it.

SHAPE NECK AND ARMHOLE

Note: Neck and armhole are shaped at the same time; please read through entire section before beg.

— *Neck Inc Row (RS):* K2, M1L, work to last 2 sts, M1R, k2—1 st inc.
— Purl 1 row.
— Rep last 2 rows 13 (14, 15, 16) (16, 16, 18) (18, 18, 18) more times. AT THE SAME TIME, when piece measures 2¾ (3¼, 3, 3½) (3¼, 3½, 4) (4¼, 4½, 4½)" / 7 (8.5, 7.5, 9) (8.5, 9, 10) (11, 11.5, 11.5) cm, beg armhole shaping as follows:

- *Armhole Inc Row 1 (RS):* Work to last 2 sts, M1R, k2—1 st inc.
- Purl 1 row.
- Rep last 2 rows 5 (5, 8, 7) (10, 11, 10) (11, 12, 12) more times.
- Rep Armhole Inc Row 1 once.
- *Armhole Inc Row 2 (WS):* P2, M1PR, work to end—1 st inc.
- Rep last 2 rows 0 (0, 0, 1) (1, 1, 2) (2, 2, 3) more time(s)—39 (41, 45, 47) (50, 53, 56) (57, 59, 62) sts when all shaping is complete.
- Do not break yarn.

BODY

- *Joining Row (RS):* Knit across left front sts, turn; using cable CO, *CO 4 (8, 10, 12) (14, 18, 22) (26, 30, 34) sts, pm in center of CO sts for side, turn;* work in pattern across back sts (beg with next row after last row worked on back); rep from * to * once, knit across right front sts—184 (200, 220, 236) (252, 272, 290) (302, 318, 338) sts.
- Work even until piece measures 3" (7.5 cm) from underarm, ending with a WS row.

SHAPE BODY

- *Inc Row (RS):* [Work to 4 sts before side marker, M1R, k2, sm, k2, M1L]

twice, knit to end—4 sts inc.
- Rep Inc Row every 14th row 4 more times—204 (220, 240, 256) (272, 292, 310) (322, 338, 358) sts.
- Work even until piece measures 12" (30.5 cm) from underarm, or to 2" (5 cm) less than desired length, ending with a WS row, dec 2 (2, 2, 0, 2, 2, 0, 0, 0, 0) sts on last row (working dec as follows: P1, p2tog, work to last 3 sts, p2tog, p1)—202 (218, 238, 256) (270, 290, 310) (322, 338, 358) sts.
- Work in Flat 2×2 Rib for 2" (4 cm).
- BO all sts in pattern.

SLEEVES

With RS facing, beg at center underarm, pick up and knit 24 (25, 26, 29) (32, 34, 37) (39, 40, 42) sts to held saddle sts, work across saddle sts in pattern (beg with next row after last row worked on saddle), pick up and knit 24 (25, 26, 29) (32, 34, 37) (39, 40, 42) sts to bottom of underarm, turn—74 (76, 78, 84) (90, 94, 100) (104, 106, 110) sts.

SHAPE CAP

Note: Do not work wraps tog with wrapped sts; they form a faux seamline along the edge of the cap.

- *Short Row 1 (WS):* Purl to 1 st before saddle sts, p2tog, work across saddle to last saddle st, p2tog, w&t—72 (74, 76, 82) (88, 92, 98) (102, 104, 108) sts.
- *Short Row 2 (RS):* Work 26 sts, w&t.
- *Short Row 3:* Work to wrapped st, p1, w&t.
- *Short Row 4:* Work to wrapped st, k1, w&t.
- Rep Short Rows 3 and 4 eighteen (19, 19, 21) (23, 23, 24) (25, 25, 26) more times, then rep Short Row 3 once more.
- *Next Row (RS):* Work to underarm; join, pm for beg of rnd, and work in the rnd as follows:

Note: Change to Circular Right and Left Diagonal Cables, beg with next rnd after last rnd worked in flat patterns.

- Work 9 (9, 8, 7) (6, 5, 5) (4, 4, 4) rnds even.
- *Dec Rnd:* K1, ssk, work to last 3 sts, k2tog, k1—2 sts dec.
- Rep last 10 (10, 9, 8) (7, 6, 6) (5, 5, 5) rnds 9 (10, 11, 12) (15, 17, 18) (20, 21, 21) more times—52 (52, 52, 56) (56, 56, 60) (60, 60, 64) sts.
- Work even until piece measures 15½ (16, 16, 16) (16½, 16½, 16½) (17, 17, 17)" [39.5 (40.5, 40.5, 40.5) (42, 42, 42) (43, 43, 43) cm] from underarm.
- Work in Circular 2×2 Rib for 2" (5 cm).
- BO all sts in pattern.

FINISHING

Weave in ends; block as desired.

FRONT BANDS/COLLAR

- With RS facing, beg at bottom of right front, pick up and knit 107 (108, 111, 114) (116, 120, 123) (127, 131, 131) sts to beg of back panel, pm, pick up and knit 48 (50, 52, 58) (58, 58, 60) (60, 60, 60) sts across back neck, pm, then pick up and knit 107 (108, 111, 114) (116, 120, 123) (127, 131, 131) sts to bottom of left front—262 (266, 274, 286) (290, 298, 306) (314, 322, 322) sts.
- Work in 2×2 Rib, beg with Row 2, for 1¼" (3 cm).

SHAPE COLLAR

- *Short Row 1 (RS):* Work to second marker, sm, work 2 sts, turn.
- *Short Row 2 (WS):* DS, work to second marker, sm, work 2 sts, turn.
- *Short Row 3:* DS, work to DS, close DS, work 4 sts, turn.
- *Short Row 4:* DS, work to DS, close DS, work 4 sts, turn.

- Rep Short Rows 3 and 4 six more times.
- *Next Row (RS):* DS, work to DS, close DS, work to end.
- Work 1 row even, closing DS as you come to it.
- *Buttonhole Row (RS):* Work 2 sts, work Single Row Buttonhole, [work 9 sts, work Single Row Buttonhole] 5 times, work to end.
- Work even until piece measures 2" (5 cm) at bottom edge, ending with a WS row.
- BO all sts in pattern.
- Sew buttons opposite buttonholes.

NUA SPORT

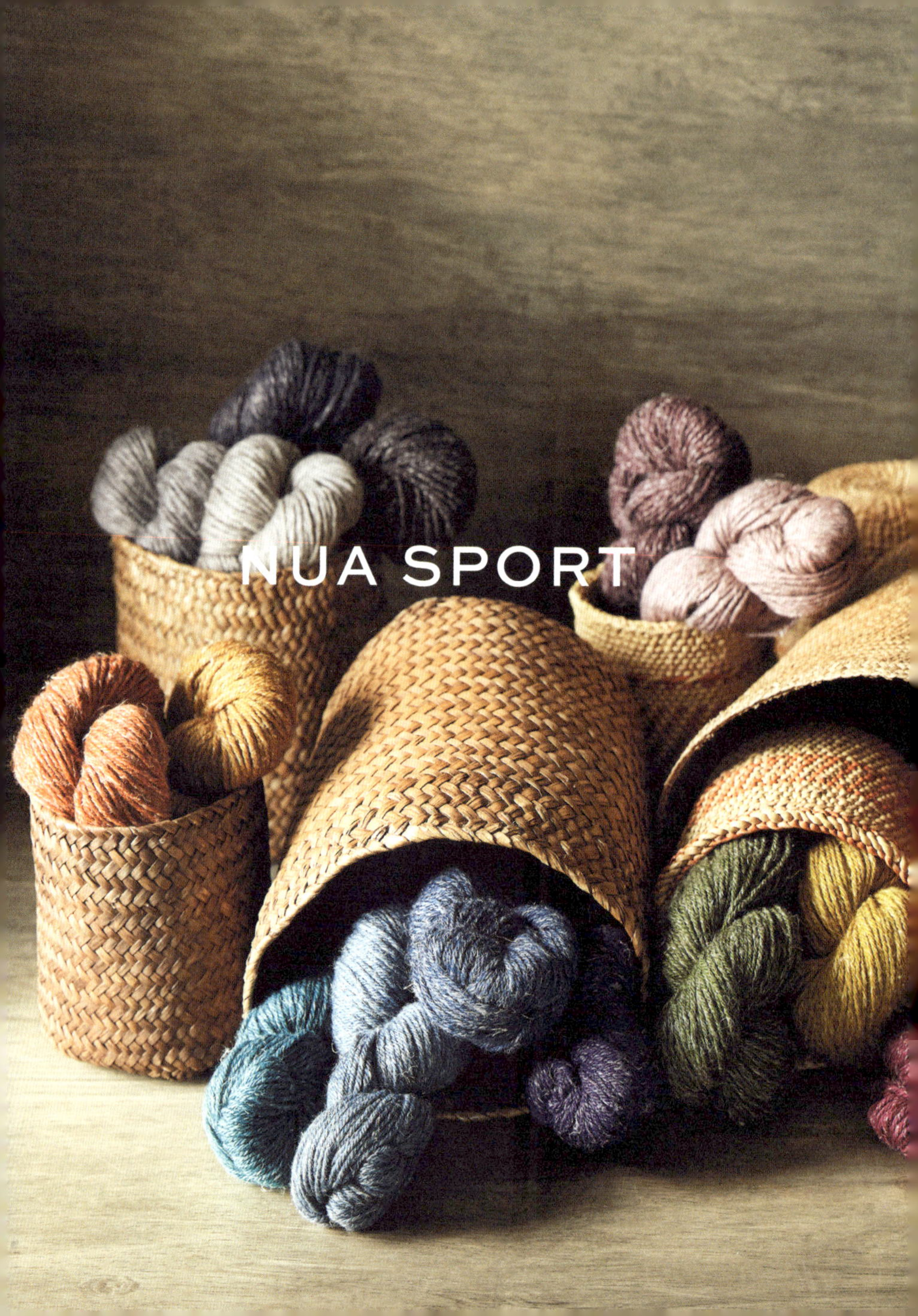

CAROL FELLER MADE GOOD USE of her studies in textile design and structural engineering when she designed this yarn called Nua Sport. Composed of three fibers—soft merino, silky yak, and sturdy linen—it is lightweight, strong, and subtly tweedy. Although "nua" means new in Irish, we have already filed it under classic. It's a true yarn for all seasons.

How did Carol arrive at this palette? She looked to nature, where she spends much of her time. She went for a mix of neutrals that stand alone, along with pots of color to complement them. Her goal was to make sure all the colors work together, allowing for easy mixing and matching. Mission accomplished!

TWINING WRAP

Design by

Carol Feller

C AROL FELLER'S LOVE OF CABLES AND TEXTURES is front and center in this long triangular wrap that easily stays put on the shoulders. Note the way the various stitch patterns dance together and become a distinctive whole with the addition of the picot border.

If you're new to cables, this is a good place to start. The shaping is minimal—all that action happens at the edges—leaving the body open for the uninterrupted twining of the stitches.

KNITTED MEASUREMENTS
Width: 70¼" (178.5 cm)
Length: 39" (99 cm)

MATERIALS
— Nua by Stolen Stitches [50 g hanks, each approx 153 yds (140 m), 60% merino wool/20% yak/20% linen]; 9 hanks Rolling Bales or Bare Necessities
— SIze US 6 (4 mm) circular needle, 32" (80 cm) long or longer, or size needed to achieve gauge
— Cable needle and stitch markers
— Blocking wires (optional)

GAUGE
27 sts and 30 rows = 4" (10 cm) over Cable Block, after blocking.
Cable Block consists of 48 stitches worked as follows: 8 sts of Twisted Cable, 16 sts of Diagonal Cable, 8 sts of Twisted Cable, then 16 sts of Padded Cable.

NOTES
This shawl is worked from narrow to wide end, with all increases worked along right edge. After you work Cable Segment 1, you'll have one Cable Block; the Cable Block consists of Twisted Cable, Diagonal Cable, Twisted Cable, then Padded Cable. To each Section of each successive Cable Segment, add one element of a new Cable Block until at the end of Section D of each Cable Segment, you'll have added an entire Cable Block. Slip all stitches purlwise, slipping with yarn to back on RS rows and with yarn to front on WS rows.

SPECIAL ABBREVIATIONS
1/1 LC (1 over 1 Left Cross): Knit second stitch through back loop, knit first and second stitches together through back loops; drop both stitches from left needle.
1/1 RC (1 over 1 Right Cross): K2tog, leaving both stitches on left needle, insert right needle between first 2 stitches on left needle and knit first stitch, then drop both stitches from left needle.
2/2 LC (2 over 2 Left Cross): Slip next 2 stitches to cable needle and hold at front of work, k2, k2 from cable needle.
2/2 RC (2 over 2 Right Cross): Slip next 2 stitches to cable needle and hold at back of work, k2, k2 from cable needle.
4/4 LC (4 over 4 Left Cross): Slip next 4 stitches to cable needle and hold at front of work, k4, k4 from cable needle.
4/4 RC (4 over 4 Right Cross): Slip next 4 stitches to cable needle and hold at back of work, k4, k4 from cable needle.

SHAWL

Set-Up

- CO 4 sts.
- *Row 1 (RS):* Sl 1, k1, yo, k2—5 sts.
- *Row 2:* Sl 1, p1, k1-tbl, p2.
- *Row 3:* Sl 1, k1, p1, yo, k2—6 sts.
- *Row 4:* Sl 1, p1, k1-tbl, k1, p2.
- *Row 5:* Sl 1, k1, p2, yo, k2—7 sts.
- *Row 6:* Sl 1, p1, k1-tbl, k2, p2.
- *Row 7:* Sl 1, k1, p2, yo, p1, k2—8 sts.
- *Row 8:* Sl 1, p1, k1, k1-tbl, k2, p2.
- *Row 9:* Sl 1, k1, p2, yo, pm, p2, k2 —9 sts.
- *Row 10:* Sl 1, p1, k2, sm, p1-tbl, k2, p2.
- *Row 11:* Sl 1, k1, p2, yo, knit to marker, sm, p2, k2—1 st inc.
- *Row 12:* Sl 1, p1, k2, sm, purl to last 5 sts, p1-tbl, k2, p2.
- *Rows 13-40:* Rep Rows 11 and 12 fourteen more times—24 sts after Row 39.

CABLE SEGMENT 1

Section A

- *Row 41 (RS):* Work Increase Panel over 4 sts (5 sts after working yo), pm, work Padded Cable over 16 sts, pm, p2, k2—1 st inc.
- *Rows 42-64:* Continue in patterns as established through Row 24 of Increase Panel—36 sts after Row 63.

Section B

- *Row 65 (RS):* Sl 1, k1, p2, yo, knit to 8 sts before marker, pm, work Twisted Cable to marker, sm, work as established to end—1 st inc.
- *Rows 66-88:* Continue in patterns as established through Row 24 of Padded Cable and inc 1 st every RS row as on Row 65—48 sts after Row 87.

Section C

- *Row 89 (RS):* Work Increase Panel over 4 sts, pm, work Diagonal Cable to marker, sm, work as established to end—1 st inc.
- *Rows 90-112:* Continue in patterns as established through Row 24 of Increase Panel—60 sts after Row 111.

Section D

- *Rows 113-136:* Repeat Section B —72 sts after Row 135.
- Cable Segment 1 is complete. You have now set up 1 full Cable Block consisting of 8 sts of Twisted Cable, 16 sts of Diagonal Cable, 8 sts of Twisted Cable, then 16 sts of Padded Cable. By the end of Section D of each of the following Cable Segments, you will have added another 48-st Cable Block.

CABLE SEGMENT 2

Section A

- *Row 137 (RS):* Work Increase Panel over 4 sts, pm, work Padded Cable to marker, sm, work as established to end—1 st inc.
- *Rows 138-160:* Continue in patterns as established through Row 24 of Increase Panel—84 sts after Row 159.

Section B

- *Row 161 (RS):* Sl 1, k1, p2, yo, knit to 8 sts before marker, pm, work Twisted Cable to marker, sm, work as established to end—1 st inc.
- *Rows 162-184:* Continue in patterns as established through Row 24 of Padded Cable; inc 1 st every RS row as on Row 161—96 sts after Row 183.

Section C

- *Rows 185 (RS):* Work Increase Panel over 4 sts (inc to 5 sts), pm, work Diagonal Cable to marker, sm, work as established to end—1 st inc.
- *Rows 186-208:* Continue in patterns as established through Row 24 of Increase Panel—108 sts after Row 207.

Section D

- *Rows 209-232:* Repeat Section B—120 sts after Row 231.

CABLE SEGMENT 3

- *Rows 233-328:* Work as for Cable Segment 2—168 sts after Row 327.

CABLE SEGMENT 4

- *Rows 329-424:* Work as for Cable Segment 2—216 sts after Row 423.

CABLE SEGMENT 5

- *Rows 425-520:* Work as for Cable Segment 2—264 sts after Row 519.

EDGING

- *Set-Up Row (RS):* Sl 1, k1, p2, yo, [k3, k2tog] 50 times (removing markers), knit to last 4 sts, p2, k2—215 sts.
- *Next Row:* Sl 1, p1, k2, knit to last 5 sts, k1-tbl, k2, p2.
- *Next Row:* Sl 1, k1, p2, yo, knit to last 4 sts, p2, k2—1 st inc.
- Rep last 2 rows 5 more times—221 sts.
- Work 1 WS row even.
- BO all sts using Picot BO: Using Cable CO, CO 2 sts, BO 6 sts, slip st from right to left needle, *using Cable CO, CO 2 sts on left needle, BO 6 sts, slip st from right to left needle; rep from * until all sts are BO. Fasten off.

FINISHING

Weave in ends. Block as desired.

STITCH PATTERNS

Increase Panel

(panel of 4 sts; inc to panel of 16 sts)

— *Row 1 (RS):* Sl 1, k1, p2, yo—5 sts.
— *Row 2:* K1-tbl, k2, p2.
— *Row 3:* Sl 1, k1, p2, yo, p1—6 sts.
— *Row 4:* K1, p1-tbl, k2, p2.
— *Row 5:* Sl 1, k1, p2, yo, k1, p1—7 sts.
— *Row 6:* K1, p1, p1-tbl, k2, p2.

Increase Panel

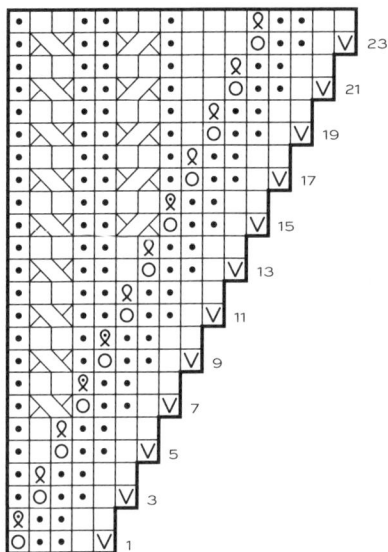

4-st panel;
inc to 16 sts

— *Row 7:* Sl 1, k1, p2, yo, 1/1 LC, p1—
  8 sts.
— *Row 8:* K1, p2, k1-tbl, k2, p2.
— *Row 9:* Sl 1, k1, p2, yo, p1, 1/1 LC,
  p1—9 sts.
— *Row 10:* K1, p2, k1, k1-tbl, k2, p2.
— *Row 11:* Sl 1, k1, p2, yo, p2, 1/1 LC,
  p1—10 sts.
— *Row 12:* K1, p2, k2, p1-tbl, k2, p2.
— *Row 13:* Sl 1, k1, p2, yo, k1, p2, 1/1 LC,
  p1—11 sts.
— *Row 14:* K1, p2, k2, p1, p1-tbl, k2, p2.
— *Row 15:* Sl 1, k1, p2, yo, 1/1 RC, p2,
  1/1 LC, p1—12 sts.
— *Row 16:* K1, p2, k2, p2, k1-tbl, k2, p2.
— *Row 17:* Sl 1, k1, p2, yo, p1, 1/1 RC, p2,
  1/1 LC, p1—13 sts.
— *Row 18:* K1, p2, k2, p2, k1, p1-tbl, k2,
  p2.
— *Row 19:* Sl 1, k1, p2, yo, k1, p1, 1/1 RC,
  p2, 1/1 LC, p1—14 sts.
— *Row 20:* K1, p2, k2, p2, k1, p1, p1-tbl,
  k2, p2.
— *Row 21:* Sl 1, k1, p2, yo, k2, p1, 1/1 RC,
  p2, 1/1 LC, p1—15 sts.
— *Row 22:* K1, p2, k2, p2, k1, p2, p1-tbl,
  k2, p2.
— *Row 23:* Sl 1, k1, p2, yo, k3, p1, 1/1 RC,
  p2, 1/1 LC, p1—16 sts.
— *Row 24:* K1, p2, k2, p2, k1, p3, p1-tbl,
  k2, p2.

Padded Cable (panel of 16 sts)

- *Rows 1, 5, 7, 9, 11, 13, 17, 19, 21, and 23 (RS):* Knit.
- *Row 2 and all WS Rows:* Purl.
- *Row 3:* 4/4 RC, 4/4 LC.
- *Row 15:* 4/4 LC, 4/4 RC.
- *Row 24:* Purl.
- Rep Rows 1–24 for Padded Cable.

Twisted Cable (panel of 8 sts)

- *Row 1 (RS):* P1, 1/1 RC, p2, 1/1 LC, p1.
- *Row 2:* K1, p2, k2, p2, k1.
- Rep Rows 1 and 2 for Twisted Cable.

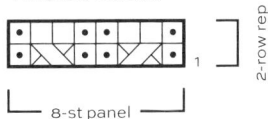

Twisted Cable

2-row rep

8-st panel

Padded Cable

23
21
19
17
15
13
11
9
7
5
3
1

24-row rep

16-st panel

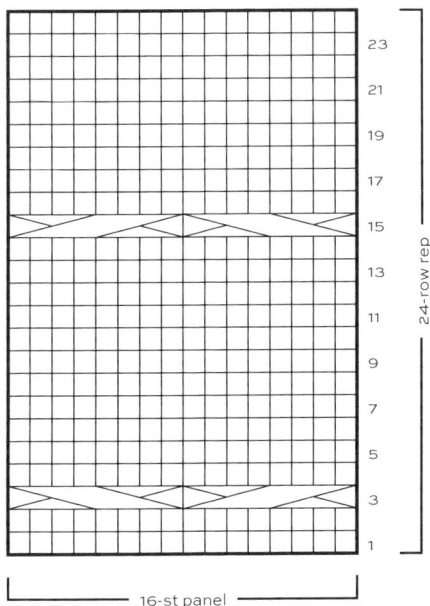

	Knit
•	Purl
ℚ	P1-tbl on WS.
ℚ	K1-tbl on WS.
V	Slip 1 purlwise wyib on RS, slip 1 purlwise wyif on WS.
O	Yo
⟋	1/1 RC
⟍	1/1 LC
	2/2 RC
	2/2 LC
	4/4 RC
	4/4 LC

Diagonal Cable (panel of 16 sts)
— *Row 1 (RS):* 2/2 LC, k12.
— *Row 2 and all WS Rows:* Purl.
— *Row 3:* K2, 2/2 LC, k10.
— *Row 5:* K4, 2/2 LC, k8.
— *Row 7:* K6, 2/2 LC, k6.
— *Row 9:* K8, 2/2 LC, k4.
— *Row 11:* K10, 2/2 LC, k2.

— *Row 13:* K12, 2/2 RC.
— *Row 15:* K10, 2/2 RC, k2.
— *Row 17:* K8, 2/2 RC, k4.
— *Row 19:* K6, 2/2 RC, k6.
— *Row 21:* K4, 2/2 RC, k8.
— *Row 23:* K2, 2/2 RC, k10.
— *Row 24:* Purl.
— Rep Rows 1–24 for Diagonal Cable.

Diagonal Cable

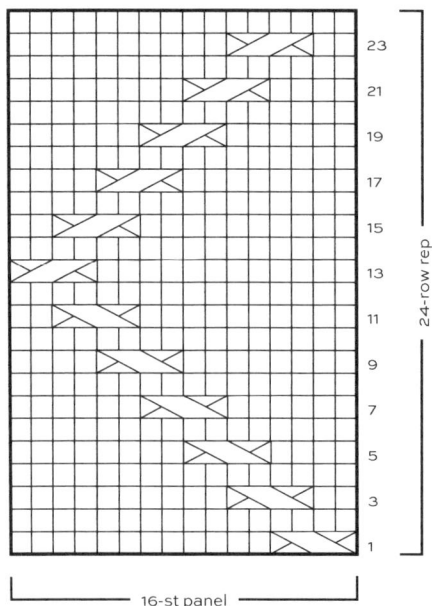

24-row rep

16-st panel

	Knit
	2/2 RC
	2/2 LC

TRELLIS TOP

Design by

Carol Feller

Given the precise engineering we associate with Carol's work, this top initially surprised us with its simple, square shape. But her signature style is here in the embossed surface design formed with a subtle lattice of cables and her novel use of buttons at the sides.

This is a multiseasonal piece to layer over T-shirts, blouses, and dresses. When choosing a size, consider what you're most likely to wear under it, then look at the finished measurements, and make your choice based on how it will fit over the layer beneath it.

KNITTED MEASUREMENTS

Bust: 33½ (38½, 44, 49) (54, 60, 65, 69½)" [85 (98, 112, 124.5) (137, 152.5, 165, 176.5) cm] buttoned

Length:20½ (21, 21, 22) (22, 23, 24, 25)" [52 (53.5, 53.5, 56) (56, 58.5, 61, 63.5) cm]

SIZE

To fit bust sizes 25-29 (30-34, 36-40, 41-45) (46-50, 52-56, 57-61, 61-65)" [63.5-73.5 (76-86.5, 91.5-101.5, 104-114.5) (117-127, 132-142, 145-155, 155-165) cm]

MATERIALS

— Nua by Stolen Stitches [50 g skeins, each approx 153 yds (140 m), 60% merino wool, 20% yak, 20% linen]: 5 (6, 7, 8) (9, 10, 11, 12) skeins Chalk and Plum
— Two size US 5 (3.75 mm) circular needles, 32" (80 cm) long, or size needed to achieve gauge
— Removable stitch markers
— Stitch holders or waste yarn
— 8 buttons, 1–1¼" (25–32 mm) diameter

GAUGE

22 sts and 33 rows = 4" (10 cm) over stockinette stitch
26 sts and 33 rows = 4" (10 cm) over Fractured Lattice Pattern

NOTES

— Back and front are worked separately from bottom up, then joined together at shoulders using a 3-needle bind-off. If you prefer, you may bind off all stitches for back and front, then sew shoulders together. The neck and body edging are worked in an applied I-cord. The pieces are worked back and forth in rows, but a circular needle is used to accommodate large number of stitches on needle. Use 2 circular needles when working body edging.
— You may work Fractured Lace Pattern from text or chart.
— You may find it helpful to place markers at each side of Fractured Lattice Panels to keep track of them.
— When working Fractured Lattice Pattern, if you do not have enough stitches to work a cable cross, work affected stitch in stockinette stitch.

SPECIAL TECHNIQUES

Applied I-Cord

*Transfer 3 I-cord stitches from right-hand needle to left-hand needle. Drawing yarn across back of knitting, k2, ssk (last I-cord stitch together with 1 picked-up stitch)

I-Cord

*Transfer 3 I-cord stitches from right-hand needle to left-hand needle. Drawing yarn across back of knitting, k3; repeat from * for specified number of rows.

I-Cord Buttonhole

Work 4 rows of I-cord, leaving stitches on right-hand needle. With yarn in back, slip 2 stitches purlwise from left- to right-hand needle, pass second stitch over first stitch, [slip 1 stitch purlwise from left- to right-hand needle, pass second stitch over first stitch] 3 times, transfer last stitch from right-hand needle back to left-hand needle.

SPECIAL ABBREVIATIONS

1/1 LC (1 over 1 Left Cross): Knit the second stitch through the back loop, knit the first and second stitches together through the back loops, then drop both stitches from the left needle.

1/1 RC (1 over 1 Right Cross): K2tog, leaving both stitches on the left needle, insert the right needle between the first 2 stitches on the left needle and knit the first stitch, then drop both stitches from the left needle.

STITCH PATTERN

Fractured Lattice Pattern
(multiple of 8 sts)
— *Row 1 (RS):* *1/1 LC, k2, 1/1 LC, 1/1 RC; rep from * to end.
— *Row 2 and all WS Rows:* Purl.
— *Row 3:* *K1, 1/1 LC, k2, 1/1 RC, k1; rep from * to end.
— *Row 5:* *1/1 RC, 1/1 LC, 1/1 RC, k2; rep from * to end.
— *Row 7:* K3, *1/1 LC, k2, 1/1 RC, k2; rep from * to last 5 sts, 1/1 LC, k3.
— *Row 8:* Purl.
— Rep Rows 1–8 for Fractured Lattice Pattern.

Fractured Lattice Pattern

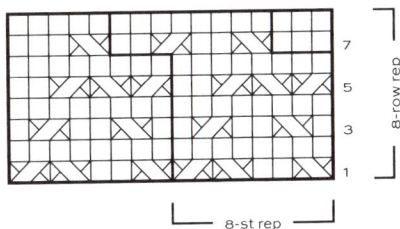

8-row rep

8-st rep

Knit on RS, purl on WS.

1/1 RC

1/1 LC

BACK

- CO 106 (122, 138, 154) (170, 186, 202, 218) sts.
- Purl 1 row.
- *Set-Up Row 1 (RS):* K1 (edge st; keep in st st), work in Fractured Lattice Pattern to last st, k1 (edge st; keep in st st).
- Continuing to work first and last sts in st st as established, work even until you have worked Rows 1–8 of Fractured Lattice Pattern twice.
- *Set-Up Row (RS):* K1, continue Fractured Lattice Pattern as established over 24 (32, 16, 24) (32, 16, 24, 32) sts, [k8, continue Fractured Lattice Pattern as established over 16 sts] 2 (2, 4, 4) (4, 6, 6, 6) times, k8, continue Fractured Lattice Pattern as established over 24 (32, 16, 24) (32, 16, 24, 32), k1.
- Continuing to work first and last sts in st st as established, work even until piece measures approx 20½ (21, 21, 22) (22, 23, 24, 25)" [52 (53.5, 53.5, 56) (56, 58.5, 61, 63.5) cm], ending with a RS row.
- *Next Row (WS):* Work 28 (35, 43, 50) (58, 64, 72, 80) sts, BO next 50 (52, 52, 54) (54, 58, 58, 58) sts, work to end. Note last row worked in Fractured Lattice Pattern. Break yarn and place sts on st holders or waste yarn.

FRONT

- Work as for Back until piece measures approx 17 (17½, 17½, 17¾) (17¾, 18, 19, 19½)" [43 (44.5, 44.5, 45) (45, 45.5, 48.5, 49.5) cm], ending with a WS row.

SHAPE RIGHT NECK EDGE

- *Next Row (RS):* Work 44 (52, 59, 67) (75, 82, 90, 98) sts and place on st holder or waste yarn for left shoulder, BO center 18 (18, 20, 20) (20, 22, 22, 22) sts, work to end—44 (52, 59, 67) (75, 82, 90, 98) sts remain for right shoulder.
- Work 1 row even.
- Working on right shoulder sts only, BO 4 sts at neck edge once, then 3 sts once—37 (45, 52, 60) (68, 75, 83, 91) sts.
- Work 1 row even.
- *Dec Row 1 (RS):* K2, ssk, work to end—1 st dec.
- *Dec Row 2:* Work to last 4 sts, ssp, p2—1 st dec.
- Rep Dec Rows 1 and 2 one (1, 1, 1) (1, 2, 2, 2) more time(s)—33 (41, 48, 56) (64, 69, 77, 85) sts.

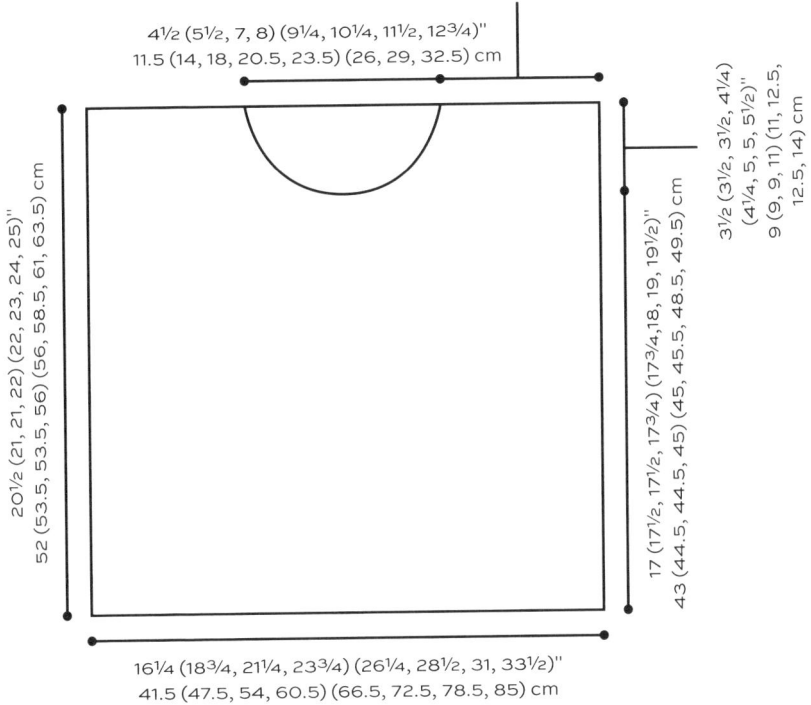

4½ (5½, 7, 8) (9¼, 10¼, 11½, 12¾)"
11.5 (14, 18, 20.5, 23.5) (26, 29, 32.5) cm

4½ (5½, 7, 8) (9¼, 10¼, 11½, 12¾)"
11.5 (14, 18, 20.5, 23.5) (26, 29, 32.5) cm

3½ (3½, 3½, 4¼) (4¼, 5, 5, 5½)"
9 (9, 9, 11) (11, 12.5, 12.5, 14) cm

20½ (21, 21, 22) (22, 23, 24, 25)"
52 (53.5, 53.5, 56) (56, 58.5, 61, 63.5) cm

17 (17½, 17½, 17¾) (17¾,18, 19, 19½)"
43 (44.5, 44.5, 45) (45, 45.5, 48.5, 49.5) cm

16¼ (18¾, 21¼, 23¾) (26¼, 28½, 31, 33½)"
41.5 (47.5, 54, 60.5) (66.5, 72.5, 78.5, 85) cm

— Rep Dec Row 1 on next RS row, then every RS row 4 (5, 4, 5) (5, 4, 4, 4) more times, working WS rows even—28 (35, 43, 50) (58, 64, 72, 80) sts.

— Work even until piece measures approx 20½ (21, 21, 22) (22, 23, 24, 25)" [52 (53.5, 53.5, 56) (56, 58.5, 61, 63.5) cm], ending with same row of Fractured Lattice Pattern as for back. Break yarn; and place sts on st holder or waste yarn.

SHAPE LEFT NECK EDGE

— With WS facing, rejoin yarn to sts on hold for left shoulder.

— BO 4 sts at neck edge once, then 3 sts once—37 (45, 52, 60) (68, 75, 83, 91) sts.

— *Dec Row 1 (RS):* Work to last 4 sts, k2tog, k2—1 st dec.

— *Dec Row 2:* P2, p2tog, work to end —1 st dec.

— Rep Dec Rows 1 and 2 one (1, 1, 1)

(1, 2, 2, 2) more time(s)—33 (41, 48, 56) (64, 69, 77, 85) sts.

— Rep Dec Row 1 on next RS row, then every RS row 4 (5, 4, 5) (5, 4, 4, 4) more times—28 (35, 43, 50) (58, 64, 72, 80) sts.

— Work even until piece measures 20½ (21, 21, 22) (22, 23, 24, 25)" [52 (53.5, 53.5, 56) (56, 58.5, 61, 63.5) cm], ending with same row of Fractured Lattice Pattern as for back. Do not break yarn.

— Place back left shoulder sts on separate needle. With RSs of pieces together, using 3-needle BO, BO shoulders as follows: Insert a third needle into front of first st on each of the 2 needles, knit 1 through both sts, *insert needle into front of next st on each of the 2 needles, knit 1 through both sts, BO 1 st; rep from * until all sts are BO.

FINISHING

Neck Edging

With RS facing, beg at right shoulder, pick up and knit approx 122 (126, 126, 134) (134, 146, 146, 146) sts evenly around neck opening. *Note*: Exact st count isn't essential. CO 3 sts at beg of left needle. *Note*: If you prefer, use waste yarn to CO the 3 I-cord sts, then graft these sts to remaining 3 sts at the end of edging. Join to work in rnd and BO sts using applied I-cord (see *Special Techniques)* until 3 sts remain. BO I-cord sts; sew beg and end of I-cord tog. If I-cord sts were CO in waste yarn, undo CO and graft I-cord ends tog.

Body Edging

— With RS facing, beginning at lower left front corner, pick up and knit 3 sts for every 4 rows and 1 st for each CO or BO st around entire edge of top. Use second circ needle when needed for the number of sts. Place 1 removable marker at each corner and 1 removable marker 72 sts up from corner markers along each side of back; buttonholes will be worked between these and corner markers. CO 3 sts at beg of left needle. *Note:* If preferred, use waste yarn to CO the 3 I-cord sts, then graft these sts to the remaining 3 sts at the end of edging. Join and work in the rnd as follows:

— Working along left edge, work applied I-cord to first buttonhole marker on left back, remove marker; work I-cord buttonhole (see *Special Techniques)* once, [work applied I-cord over next 18 sts, work I-cord

buttonhole] 3 times, work applied I-cord over next 2 sts, remove corner marker, work 2 rows of I-cord to ease I-cord around corner; work applied I-cord to corner marker, remove marker, work 2 rows of I-cord to turn corner; work applied I-cord over next 2 sts, work I-cord buttonhole, [work applied I-cord over next 18 sts, work I-cord buttonhole] 3 times, remove marker; work applied I-cord to end, working 2 rows of I-cord at corner markers to turn corners.

— BO I-cord sts and sew beg and end of I-cord tog. If I-cord sts were CO in waste yarn, undo CO and graft I-cord ends tog. Weave in ends. Block as desired.

LAYERING

WHEN I WAS A KID, we had outfits. My tan corduroy slacks (yes we called them slacks) with my brown checked shirt and tan corduroy safari jacket—that was a cute outfit, just the thing for a girl in a Dorothy Hamill haircut.

The outfit was the outfit. You didn't break it up into its components and mix them with pieces from another outfit, such as the pinwale navy corduroy jumper dress (in the '70s we wore corduroy, OK?) over a floral print short-sleeved blouse. That would have been layering, and that was not a thing that we did then.

But now we are layerers, especially if we're knitters. We have sweaters we wear on their own and then, when the weather and/or personal style dictates, we add underlayers and overlayers, or hats and scarves. With layers, we can play with proportion and color in wondrous ways. Add just the right layer and, all of a sudden, a ho-hum jeans and shirt combo skews rock-and-roll or equestrian—depending on your plans for the day.

—Kay

ARCADE CAP

Design by

Carol Feller

THIS CHIC LITTLE BEANIE FEATURES a quartet of graceful arches that emerge out of the ribbing. Another designer might have added more arches around the circumference, but Carol is a master of restraint, knowing just when to stop to strike the perfect note of sophistication.

Every knitter will want to take this off your head to examine how it's made!

KNITTED MEASUREMENTS

Circumference: 17½ (18¾, 20, 21½)"
[44.5 (47.5, 51, 54.5) cm]
Length: 7½ (7¾, 8¼, 8½)" [19 (19.5, 21, 21.5) cm]

SIZES

Small (Medium, Large, X-Large)
To fit head circumference: 20½ (21¾, 23, 24½)" [52 (55, 58.5, 62) cm]

MATERIALS

— Nua by Stolen Stitches [50 g skeins,
  each approx 153 yds (140 m), 60%
  merino wool, 20% yak, 20% linen]:
  1 (1, 2, 2) skein(s) Cerebellum
— Size US 4 (3.5 mm) circular needle,
  16" (40 cm) long, and double-
  pointed needles (set of 4 or 5), or
  size needed to achieve gauge
— Stitch markers
— Cable needle

GAUGE

24 sts and 37 rows = 4" (10 cm) over
reverse stockinette stitch

NOTE

The hat is worked in the round from the
bottom up. You may work the Cable
pattern from the text or the chart.

SPECIAL ABBREVIATIONS

2/1 LPC (2 over 1 Left Purl Cross): Slip
the next 2 stitches to cable needle and
hold at front of work, p1, k2 from cable
needle.

2/1 RPC (2 over 1 Right Purl Cross): Slip
the next stitch to cable needle and hold
at back of work, k2, p1 from cable needle.

2/2 LPC (2 over 2 Left Purl Cross): Slip
the next 2 stitches to cable needle and
hold at front of work, p2, k2 from cable
needle.

2/2 RPC (2 over 2 Right Purl Cross): Slip
the next 2 stitches to cable needle and
hold at back of work, k2, p2 from cable
needle.

Dec3: Slip 1 stitch purlwise, knit 2
stitches together, pass slipped stitch
over, slip stitch from right to left needle,
pass second stitch over slipped stitch,
then slip stitch back to the right needle.
Three stitches have been decreased.

Dec4: With yarn in back, slip 2 stitches
one at a time purlwise, purl 1, take yarn to
back and leave it there, [pass one slipped
stitch over purled stitch on right needle
then slip that stitch back to left needle,
pass second stitch on left needle over
first stitch then slip resulting stitch back
to right needle] twice. Four stitches have
been decreased.

HAT

BRIM
— Using circular needle, CO 112 (120, 128, 136) sts. Join, being careful not to twist sts; pm for beg of rnd and work in the rnd as follows:
— Work in 2×2 Rib for 2" (5 cm).

BODY
— *Set-Up Rnd:* P40 (44, 48, 52), pm, [k2, p2] 7 times, k2, pm, purl to end.
— Work even in established pattern until piece measures 2¾ (3, 3½, 3¾)" [7 (7.5, 9, 9.5) cm].
— *Set-Up Rnd:* Purl to marker, sm, work Arch Cable to marker, sm, purl to end.
— Work even until Arch Cable is complete, removing markers on either side of pattern on final rnd—97 (105, 113, 121) sts.

CROWN
Note: Change to dpns when necessary for number of sts on needle.
— *Set-Up Rnd:* [P12 (13, 14, 15), pm] 7 times, p11 (12, 13, 14), p2tog—96 (104, 112, 120) sts.
— *Dec Rnd 1:* *P1, p2tog-tbl, purl to 3 sts before marker, p2tog, p1, sm; rep from * to end—16 sts dec.

— *Next Rnd:* Purl.
— Rep last 2 rnds 3 (3, 4, 4) more times, removing all markers except beg-of-rnd marker on last rnd—32 (40, 32, 40) sts.

For Sizes Small and Large:
— *Dec Rnd 2:* *P2tog-tbl, p2tog; rep from * to end—16 sts.
— *Next Rnd:* Purl.
— *Dec Rnd 3:* *P2tog; rep from * to end—8 sts.

For Sizes Medium and X-Large:
— *Dec Rnd 2:* *P1, p3tog, p1; rep from * to end—24 sts.
— *Next Rnd:* Purl.
— *Dec Rnd 3:* *P3tog; rep from * to end—8 sts.

All Sizes
Cut yarn, leaving 6" (15 cm) tail; thread tail through rem sts, pull tight, and fasten off.

FINISHING
Weave in ends. Block as desired.

STITCH PATTERNS

2×2 Rib (multiple of 4 sts)
— *All Rnds:* *K2, p2; rep from * to end.

Arch Cable (panel of 30 sts; dec to panel of 15 sts)
— *Rnd 1:* [K2, p2] 3 times, 2/1 LPC, 2/1 RPC, [p2, k2] 3 times.
— *Rnd 2:* [K2, p2] twice, k2, p3, k4, p3, [k2, p2] twice, k2.
— *Rnd 3:* [K2, p2] twice, k2, p3, dec3, p3, [k2, p2] twice, k2—27 sts.
— *Rnds 4–6:* [K2, p2] twice, k2, p7, [k2, p2] twice, k2.
— *Rnd 7:* [K2, p2] twice, 2/1 LPC, p5, 2/1 RPC, [p2, k2] twice.
— *Rnd 8:* K2, p2, k2, p3, k2, p5, k2, p3, k2, p2, k2.
— *Rnd 9:* K2, p2, k2, p3, 2/2 LPC, p1, 2/2 RPC, p3, k2, p2, k2.

— *Rnd 10:* K2, p2, k2, p5, dec4, p5, k2, p2, k2—23 sts.
— *Rnds 11–14:* K2, p2, k2, p11, k2, p2, k2.
— *Rnd 15:* K2, p2, 2/1 LPC, p9, 2/1 RPC, p2, k2.
— *Rnd 16:* K2, p3, k2, p9, k2, p3, k2.
— *Rnd 17:* K2, p3, 2/2 LPC, p5, 2/2 RPC, p3, k2.
— *Rnd 18:* [K2, p5] 3 times, k2.
— *Rnd 19:* K2, p5, 2/2 LPC, p1, 2/2 RPC, p5, k2.
— *Rnd 20:* K2, p7, dec4, p7, k2—19 sts.
— *Rnds 21–24:* K2, p15, k2.
— *Rnd 25:* 2/1 LPC, p13, 2/1 RPC.
— *Rnd 26:* P1, k2, p13, k2, p1.
— *Rnd 27:* P1, 2/2 LPC, p9, 2/2 RPC, p1.
— *Rnd 28:* P3, k2, p9, k2, p3.
— *Rnd 29:* P3, 2/2 LPC, p5, 2/2 RPC, p3.
— *Rnd 30:* [P5, k2] twice, p5.
— *Rnd 31:* P5, 2/2 LPC, p1, 2/2 RPC, p5.
— *Rnd 32:* P7, dec4, p7—15 sts.

Arch Cable

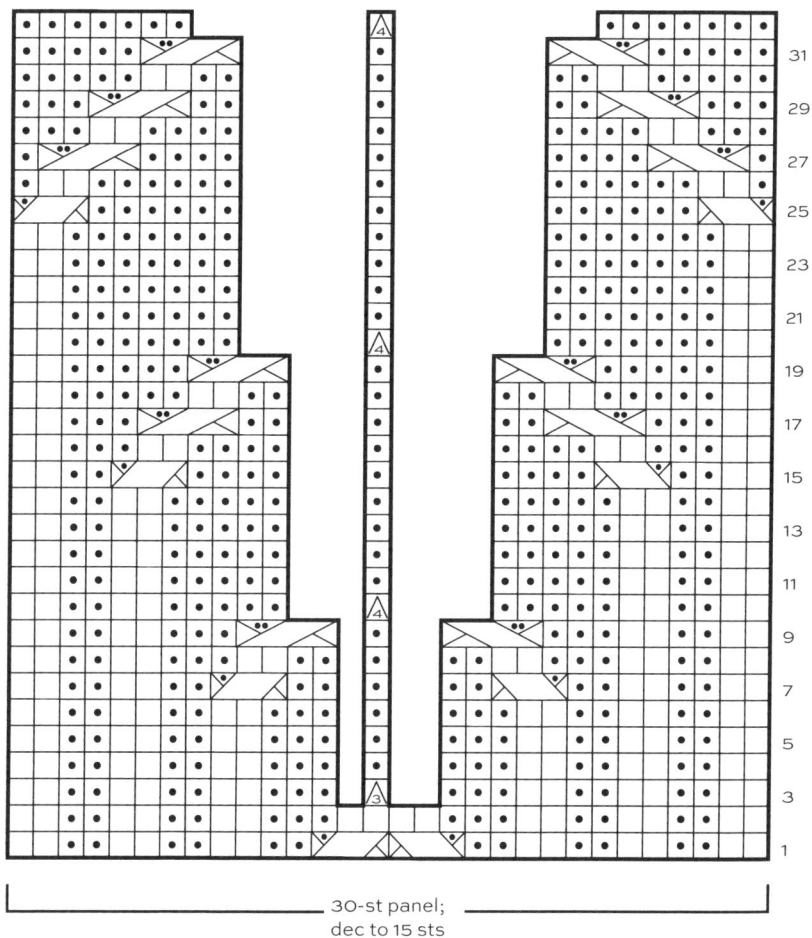

31
29
27
25
23
21
19
17
15
13
11
9
7
5
3
1

30-st panel;
dec to 15 sts

☐ Knit	◤ ▱	2/1 RPC
◉ Purl	▱ ◥	2/1 LPC
/3\ Dec3	◤◤ ▱	2/2 RPC
/4\ Dec4	▱ ◥◥	2/2 LPC

ABBREVIATIONS

Approx:	Approximately
Beg:	Begin(ning)(s)
BO:	Bind off
CO:	Cast on
Dec:	Decreas(ed)(es)(ing)
Dpn:	Double-pointed needle(s)
Inc:	Increas(ed)(es)(ing)
K:	Knit
K2tog:	Knit 2 stitches together. One stitch has been decreased.
K3tog:	Knit 3 stitches together. Two stitches have been decreased.
P3tog:	Purl 3 stitches together. Two stitches have been decreased.
P:	Purl
P2tog:	Purl 2 stitches together. One stitch has been decreased.
Pm:	Place marker
Rep:	Repeat(ed)(ing)(s)
Rnd(s):	Round(s)
RS:	Right side
Sl:	Slip
Sm:	Slip marker
Ssk:	Slip 1 stitch knitwise, slip 1 stitch purlwise, insert left needle into the front of these 2 stitches and knit them together from this position. One stitch has been decreased.
St st:	stockinette stitch
St(s):	Stitch(es)
Tbl:	Through the back loop(s)
Tog:	Together
WS:	Wrong side
Wyib:	With yarn in back
Wyif:	With yarn in front
Yo:	Yarnover